I0791362

SHAMING

MOOD SWINGS

"MYSTERIOUS"

"COMPLEX"

OVERLY
ATTENTIVE

"SPONTANEOUS"

BLAMING

ACCUSING

SOUND FAMILIAR??

These words describing one single person can be a disastrous, and likely dangerous situation.

- Oh, he's JUST a "spontaneous" person

- Oh, he's JUST a "mysterious" person

- Oh, he's JUST a "complicated" person

- Oh, he's JUST always trying to help others and

  always gets burned

- Oh, he JUST had a tough life growing up

- Oh, he's JUST tired of people not doing things

  right, even me

- Oh, he's JUST sick of his "friends" "using" him

- Oh, he's JUST moody sometimes…

I AM <u>NOT</u>:

A DOCTOR,

PSYCHOLOGIST,

SOCIOLOGIST, or

PSYCHIATRIST

What I AM

is someone who dealt with an alleged Sociopath for over 10 years. I am writing this pocket guide as a complete layman. This is what I wish I had known.

Trapped - beyond belief; beyond help; beyond reason. Trapped in a web of lies, deceit, threats, and fear. Trapped with no way out but to start from scratch with nothing. I was too young to know any signs. Too sheltered. Gleaming with youth, hope, and determination. Then, I met him. The truth of a troubled youth was hidden from me by all. The truth of an evil soul only happy when manipulating and twisting reality. A web bigger than myself; I felt alone. However, internet searches, over 10 years of research on sociopaths, and social media groups showed me quite the opposite. If only I had known the signs –

THE

RED

FLAGS

SHORT LIST:

1. LIAR

They tell blatant lies – whether small or big. Even if a sociopath must make something up, they will. It's all about convincing people of what they want them to believe or what they want them to do.

2. NO CARE FOR THE TRUTH

This is different than lying. They deny they ever said or did something, even though you have proof. Most people finally figuring out that they've gotten involved with a sociopath will start to write down or record incidents. It doesn't matter because the sociopath will "brush it off" – even with recordings or written texts or emails.

3. SPITEFUL

They use what is near and dear to you as ammunition against you. Once the 'charming' stage is over and they've learned about your struggles in your life, they will begin to throw them in your face. If you've shared intimate details of your life, they will use them later to upset you, manipulate you, or both.

4. ENERGY DRAINING

They wear you down over time. Nothing is ever good enough. If you do 'A' "YOU SHOULD'VE DONE 'B!!'" and if you do 'B' "YOU SHOULD'VE DONE 'A'!" A sociopath will attack you for not doing the opposite of whatever you do. You can't win. If you end up proving them wrong, then they accuse you of "being perfect" in a nasty tone. "I'm sorry I'm not PERFECT like you." "Oh, you're just perfect."

5. DECEITFUL

Their actions do not match their words.

6. GIVING AFTER BEING "MEAN"

They will say what they think you want to hear so that you either believe them or forgive them. Broken promises, along with impromptu gifts or actions will aide in this continuing cycle of abuse and forgiveness. They throw in positive reinforcement to confuse you. Once they feel they've been forgiven, they will go back to their sociopathic ways. Note: A sociopath will also almost never do something without wanting or demanding something in return. Everything is about them, even if it looks like it's for or about you.

7. CONSTANTLY CHANGES MIND

They know confusion weakens people. It's also hard to live a smooth life when you are forced to constantly "readjust" plans. They may also throw in impromptu plans if you tell them that you have plans with others. This will come as trying to outdo your plans with "bigger, better" plans that they already had or were going to "surprise" you with even though they have not. This may be considered by you as "spontaneous."

8. PROJECTION

They project (accuse you of what they do) – cheating, lying, any bad habits that they have; it will be said that you have them.

9. FALSE BETRAYAL

They try to align people against you. They will tell their family (usually enablers that will defend them because of their lies and previous gaslighting) and anyone they know or anyone that both of you know small lies about you to build a "case" for later.

10. GASLIGHTING

They start telling you or others that you are crazy or you are not who you seem to be.
This is one of the most effective tools of the "Gaslighter," because it is dismissive. The gaslighter knows if they try to make you question your sanity, people will not believe you when you tell them the gaslighter is abusive or out-of-control. It is a master technique.

11. DISHONEST

They tell you everyone else is a liar and will say or do anything to try to make their lies truth. Most likely, they are not faithful. They will tell other women that they are not married, not involved, or only involved with you because you share children together.

12. IRRITABLE, JUDGMENTAL, IRRATIONAL

They begin to constantly critique your every move and word. They are elated to point out any mistakes you make and capitalize on them by bashing you relentlessly – even for the smallest error; like missing a turn while driving. You may begin to feel anxiety and eventually that you must "tip-toe" around this person. It seems to be a "power" move to try to show you why they are smarter or more capable than you, REGARDLESS of if you are or aren't. They also over-react to small issues and may under-react to large issues.

13. LACK OF PROBLEM-SOLVING SKILLS

Most of the time they will choose to discard something rather than work through a problem - whether it is a job, relationship, or a problem in general. They do not have foresight to figure out solutions. This will generally lead them to discard or make up lies if any reasoning is necessary. This will also be the reason that a sociopath has a hard time keeping a steady job. They may change companies, start new businesses often (then just suddenly stop or close it), and not commit to anything.

14. MANIPULATIVE

They make a routine of manipulating situations in order to make themselves look like an overall better person than those around them. Example: getting ready for an "impromptu" outing ahead of time while alerting the rest of their family or party at the last minute about the outing. The sociopath will then tell the other party that they are always running late or take forever while the sociopath is fully ready to walk out of the door. My experience estimates that the purpose of this is to project their issues onto others. Sociopaths tend to have daily trouble getting themselves in order, including getting groomed and dressed for the day.

15. CHARMING – YES, CHARMING

This should be number ONE as a red flag. If a sociopath started out doing numbers 1-14, they'd never succeed. <u>THERE IS NOTHING WRONG WITH A LITTLE CHARM.</u> However, <u>excessive</u>, <u>REPEATED</u>, <u>OVER-AGGRESSIVE</u> charm and compliments CAN be your number one RED FLAG to start paying attention to other habits, words, and actions. He will be charming, OVERLY attentive, and completely "into you" in the beginning to "win you over." He will listen intently in order to learn your weaknesses. He will revel your abilities – at first. You can do no wrong. Then, little by little, the cycle will begin. They may try to isolate you from your friends and family. You will be their scapegoat (blame) for EVERYTHING. They will start calling you names, calling you stupid, questioning your actions with name calling, and maybe even threaten your livelihood, safety, or your actual life.

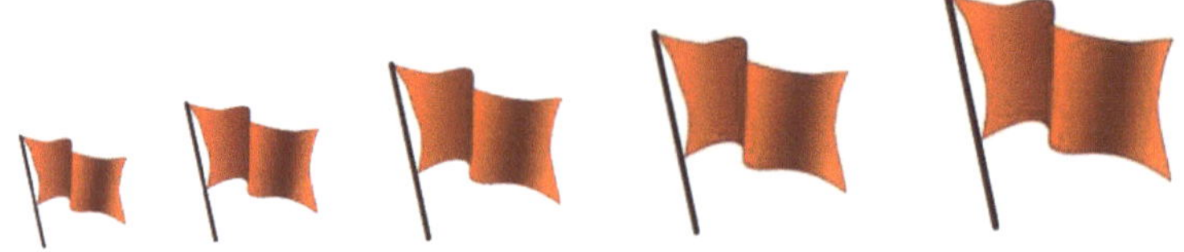

This is just a synopsis of experiences that may happen in similar situations. One thing that somehow surprises some is how others' experiences are NEARLY IDENTICAL. Women from different backgrounds, ethnicities, financial situations, etc.… There ARE female sociopaths, however, these observations are from my personal perspective with dealing with a purported sociopath. It seems though there is something about sociopaths that makes people think that they are just individually complicated people for whatever reason. "Just different." NO – MOST ARE THE SAME. Their "episodes" of mental breakdowns and shouting are similar. Their threats of leaving you broke and homeless are similar. Their threats of "No one else will put up with you," "You'll never find someone else," "Who would want YOU?!!" are ALL SIMILAR. Sociopaths are complicated; until they're not.

OTHER NOTES AND OBSERVATIONS:

Sociopaths often have cycles. They may physically act out (not always ON a person) - but, by throwing things, punching things, or trying to "look" terrifying to scare people into submission.

After an episode, they may try extremely hard to do or say things to make you forgive them. There will be some sort of excuse of why they behaved that way. NOTE – THERE IS NEVER AN EXCUSE FOR VIOLENCE OR ABUSE. Abuse can be emotional, verbal, financial, or physical.

In my personal experience, I was subjected to a lot of emotional, verbal, and financial abuse. Although I was quite aware of this, I felt extremely trapped in my situation. My options were close to zero.

Sociopaths are also drawn to "friends" who have little to no morals, values, respect for others, etc. They recognize and value these people lacking morals because their own lack of morals remains unchecked; never being judged by those who are just as devious.

Sociopaths dismiss good people as "lame" or belittle them and their successes (mild gaslighting).

Sociopaths seem to take what they know are bad traits or feelings about themselves and project them onto a victim. They are sickened with envy, especially if they naturally have a starting advantage of those they envy. These include growing up in privilege or having a higher position of power. A sociopath will almost always attempt to be in a position of higher power. They aim to control as many people as possible and act like a King. We can see publicly what a Dictator does. However, the little things or private moments are often not publicly known.

According to psychiatrists, there is no cure for a sociopath. They will victimize people their entire lives. They feel that nothing is wrong with them and that **others** are <u>always</u> the problem. After they have destroyed you, they will seek out their next victim. If you have already been involved with a sociopath, you are not "a sucker," "dumb," "gullible," or any "shameful" thing. Sociopaths try to attach themselves to people whom they can use. Once they feel or see that they can no longer use you, they will make any attempt to discredit you and leave you.

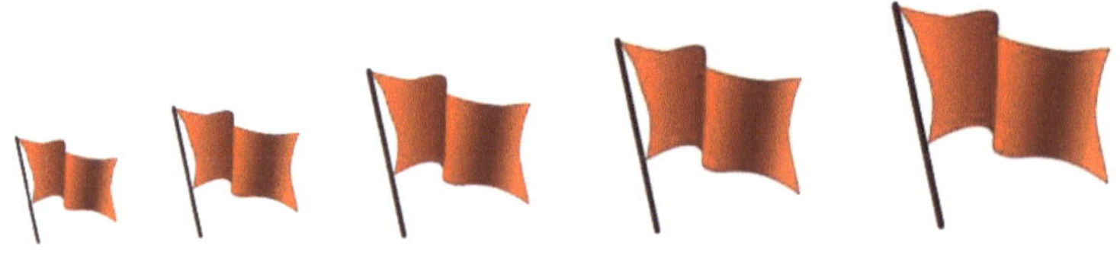

Please do not try to change them or think that it will be different with you. They lack sincerity and emotion; only mimicking what they've observed from others.

If you are being abused, please seek help from a professional.

The best advice that can be given is to GET OUT AND SEEK HELP. There are local services available that may be able to help you heal from any ordeals that you find yourself dealing with in life.

This small guide is merely to show that women do not have to feel alone or ashamed in some cases. I have found that many women will carry this secret forever. I hope to see more women seek help from a trusted source. I hope to see more women thrive and fulfill their life purpose. I hope to see more women lift each other and form true, caring sisterhoods. I hope to see more women lift the weight off of their shoulders…

And – JUST BREATHE.

WEB OF LIES, GASLIGHTING, & MANIPULATION

MY STORY:

It's hard to know where to start. I've thought about starting from the beginning of my existence; however, my story is not unique. So, I'll just start with a basic background of my life before I met him. I am the youngest of my siblings. My Father died unexpectedly in my early years. My Mother was in a depression for most of the time afterwards. Although not physically neglected, I was woefully emotionally neglected. I've been told since that a complete person has been loved and nurtured. I was not shown this. I found comfort in friends, other relatives, and extracurricular school activities. I achieved enough accolades to have a strong sense of self-esteem and accomplishment.

Fast forward to my first Summer semester in college. was fresh out of a relationship and had no interest in beginning another one. I also was set to leave the Country to attend an International university in a couple of months.

Thinking back to my fresh, new beginning at the age of 17, I was a bright-eyed ambitious girl. I was ready to make my mark on the World. That summer was about getting out of the house and being around other college students. I only signed up for a few classes, so I had ample free time to enjoy the spoils of freedom. I enjoyed meeting new people in my new college town.

One day, I was introduced to a guy by a mutual friend. This guy had an obnoxiously bright painted car that caught my attention nearly before he did. As I commented on the "loud, tacky car" parked on the street, both the guy and mutual friend laughed loudly. Then, I was told that it was the guy's car.

⚑   That should've been a RED FLAG. He was an attention seeking person who wanted to draw people – good or bad reaction – to him.

*These red flags that will be placed throughout this book are in hindsight. These are the things that should have

After chatting, we all ended up going to run errands. I was quite comfortable, as I knew the mutual friend very well. We went to return a movie that was due back at Blockbuster, grabbed a snack, then ended up going to the guy's house to hang out for a bit. When we reached his house, he and our mutual friend said that they were working on something and insisted that I go to dinner with his parents. This was a very odd moment for me, but I really didn't feel like I had a choice. I later (months later) found out that they just wanted to smoke weed and didn't want me to know. I was a pretty straightlaced person and they knew I wouldn't partake in that.

So, after some pressure from both guys, I folded and accompanied his parents (whom I just met) for dinner.

We went to a Chinese buffet in their town. As I was choosing my food, his Mother came up to me and spoke very quietly to me. I did not understand her, as she was whispering. I apologized and asked her to repeat herself, but she looked up at her approaching husband and declined; saying never mind. That could have saved me. One sentence could have turned how my whole life going forward went. We'll come back to that later. We ate, then returned to their home. Soon after, I was brought back to my dorm.

That summer I got my first job. I was excited and happy to be busy going to class and working at my favorite store in the local mall. In between classes and work, the new guy came to visit me frequently. On our first outing alone, he told me that he was 21 and that his Dad wasn't' his 'real Dad." He said that his real Dad was Hispanic and that I had met his Stepdad. I didn't think anything of it, so I didn't say anything. His Mother called me often to invite me to lunch.

More and more time was spent with this new guy. We'
go to dinner and to the mall. There wasn't too much
more to do in our college town. Our first time at the ma
together, I picked out outfits and we walked to the
register. He attempted to pay for my finds, but I said
"no" and that I had my own credit cards that my Mom
paid while I was in school. Being 17 years old, I'd neve
had a guy take me shopping at that point. He seemed
disappointed, but I insisted that I pay for my own
purchases.

⚑ Overly charming or over-stepping boundaries is a
RED FLAG.

The summer went on and everything flowed well. Soo
it was time for me to start my university venture
overseas. I was excited. I had been clear from the
beginning that I was only there for the summer. The
weekend before I was set to leave for my new school,
he invited me to go to another state for the weekend
with his family. I was open to going, but my Mother

insisted that I did not. This was going to be a big move for me, so she didn't want me to tire myself.

The time came for my departure. I said my goodbyes and was off. I enjoyed exploring and learning about different cultures. I met a lot of exciting people and even a few celebrities. I kept in touch with the new guy calling him sometimes from the shared hallway. I wrote letters sometimes also. I was focused on school and maintaining a 4.0 GPA. However, after I turned 18, I became homesick. The country that I was living in became a bit tedious to navigate and the university accommodations were not what I expected. The school moved from dorms to hotels and hostiles right before my arrival. So, I made the decision to return home.

Upon my return, I called friends to let them know I had returned. I called the new guy. He was surprised to hear that I was back. He didn't sound as enthused as before I left. I felt that was okay because I had previously made it clear that I would not be returning home. After a couple of days, we met up. It was the

busy holiday season. We went on random dates but did
not discuss being in an actual exclusive relationship.

After the holidays, I reached out to an old high school
crush. We began speaking daily; however, he was in
another state. I felt that the new guy wasn't interested
in a relationship although I was ready for a boyfriend
again. After a few months, I ended up moving to the old
crush's state. That lasted for about 6 months due
mostly to us not agreeing on responsibilities. Then,
once again, I returned home.

It took a couple of months to reach back out to the new
guy. This time, though, we walked more on a friendship
line than a relationship line. I even offered to set him up
with a crush that he had. This immediately sparked a
bit of jealousy in me. So, I added myself as an option to
be set up with him. I told him that I really was beginning
to have feelings for him. He "happily" chose me. I was
happy. I was also relieved that someone else would not
be taking him away from me. I'd grown attached to him

We laughed a lot. I enjoyed his family's dynamic of both parents and family dinners. He was kind and overly attentive to me. He went out of his way for me. I felt cherished and loved.   Although I enjoyed our time together, neither of us were in school. Our days were filled with just hanging out around his house and town. He randomly worked for his Dad, which I found out was NOT his Stepdad, but his actual (<u>NOT</u> Hispanic) Dad. He told me that I misunderstood him. His Dad's Mother had close family friends that were Hispanic. They called them Aunt and Uncle. So, he insisted that I was confused.

🚩 Changing life stories or what someone has said or claimed is a RED FLAG. Insisting that YOU misunderstood or misheard what they said is considered gaslighting.

After a while it was time for me to get back on track with school. I'd taken some time off to see what I wanted to major in since I'd left my International school. I ended up leaving my state again and going to live with a close relative to attend a college there. This was the best option for me at the time. The "not so new anymore" guy came to visit me in between a working trip. Let's see. I'll give him the name "the guy." So, the guy came to visit during an unexpected blizzard layover. We spent part of the night together in his hotel room. Then, said our goodbyes again.

Soon after, I was again ready to go home. I hated the weather and missed my friends. Again, the guy and I began spending time together. However, my time was short lived at home. I decided to move back to another state and once again start at another college.

⚑   I want to add that my inconsistency and roaming were probably an attractive feature to a sociopath. My own instability and lack of parental and family support may have made me a target. Sociopaths like adventurous, busy people. They also like people with

I started school and leased a condo in the new city. I was settled and becoming more responsible. The guy came to visit often. I also went to visit him. I went on a trip to visit my sister and he ended up staying at my condo during that time. He attempted to move in with me, but I told him that I needed to learn to live alone and focus on school. I think that he felt this as a rejection to him. I've since learned that rejection is very insulting to a sociopath.

The stance he chose to take was to pull back on our relationship. Eventually, though, he decided to begin taking steps to move forward in his life; enrolling in a school across the Country. After some thought and me feeling that I did not want to end the relationship, I decided to move with him. This is the very moment I put myself in a dependent situation. This is a sociopath's dream come true. They aim to have their victims completely dependent on them.

We moved to another state together. It was a new experience actually living together. We were both busy starting new schools, so the atomsphere was pretty calm. We ended up getting a dog because he'd always had one. The new puppy had a hard time adjusting and cried often at first. One night he put the puppy in a closet because he didn't want to deal with it. I swiftly took the puppy and laid it on my chest to soothe it. I ended up just sleeping with the puppy on my chest so that it could feel my heartbeat. That should have been a sign.

🚩   There are cases where sociopaths will be abusive or do things like this to animals. You really must pay attention to the way someone treats animals as well as other people other than yourself.

After a while, he started spending more time with classmates. We went to a party at someone's house and they offered me drugs. I declined and said that I didn't do that. He got embarrased, but I stood my ground.

🚩   Sociopaths often have substance abuse problems. They may hide it at first, but will eventually not be able to hide their bad habits if the relationship continues.

We were in college, so I dismissed it as something he was doing as a college-aged phase. As you can see, the red flags were popping up more often. Had I known what to look for, I could've known that it was time to end the relationship for good. However, growing up so sheltered but with very little nurturing; I was naïve. So, I continued on with this relationship. One more move to yet another college was upcoming. He started to hear from people that the college he chose was not appropriately accredited, nor did they have a good path to a an actual career. He hadn't researched it properly.

The next move, across the Country again, lasted abou
a year. We both completed our college terms at this
time. There were several instances that should have
ended this relationship, but I felt that I was too
committed and had already put in so much effort. I
dismissed it as stress, moodiness, my own fault of not
being adequate enough of a partner, etc… A sociopat
will always turn the blame to you. It's always your faul
even when it's not. At this point, I was always just tryir
to please him and believed his criticism of me and
others. Every decision I made was based on whether

thought he would approve or not. He would want me to wear my hair a certain way, dress in certain clothes, and tried to push me to get breast implants. He wanted to control every facet of my life.

🚩   Sociopaths are obsessed with control. They want a willing victim that will allow them to control everything they possibly can. They will start weighing in on your physical appearance, clothing, friends, family, job, what you discuss, and every other thing possible. They will do it in a suggestive (manipulative) way. They may point out other people as an example. It's a way to build their own personal fantasyland of their own making.

I am a very headstrong person. However, the manipulation was so subtle at times that I didn't realize that I was being molded into the version of what he wanted me to be. Sometimes I would disagree with his wishes. In those cases, he would begin criticizing me and my choices. Most of the time I would just give in to his wishes.

Fast forwarding to after college, we moved back to the state that I was in before we moved in together. I got a job and he started a business with the help of his family. The Christmas prior, we got engaged. This was only after I told him that I wasn't going to pressure him but I also wasn't going to waste away my twenties in a relationship going nowhere. I believe that his actual decision came after Christmas when friends asked him what he gave me for Christmas. I don't remember if had given me anything or not. But, he told his friends that he had something planned. Later that day he brought me into a jewelry store and told me to pick a ring. Then, in the parking lot, he handed me the bag and said "here." I stupidly took the bag. Later that night, I mentioned that he didn't even propose. So, he got down on one knee and did. Romantic, huh? This is where the lack of nurturing growing up showed it's ugly head. I should've realized that this would be how my life would be if I moved forward with him. No real emotions or real love. No real acts of romance or loving interest.

So, back to the move after college. One night we went out to celebrate a friend at a club. He accused me of flirting with someone; although I did not. He was not next to me at the time, but got very angry. When I was back with him he stormed off and attempted to leave me there at the club. I hurriedly caught up with him. He began yelling at me and repeatedly hit me on the back of my head; screaming at me to get in the car. I was in shock. I did get in the car. As soon as we got back home, I started packing my things. It was very late. I waited until the morning, then loaded up my car and left. He called me repeatedly, but I did not answer. I finally answered so I could focus on driving. He was in a panic. He kept saying that we were supposed to meet up with his parents for a late lunch later that day. He said he didn't know what to tell them. He began pleading with me. He knew exactly what to say to me. He knew that one of my weak spots was a family unit. He knew that I was comforted by the inclusion of his parents and family. He knew that I craved a solid family bond – with 2 parents, family dinners, and closeness. He knew what I lacked. He'd paid attention to the things I said and to the things I liked. I'd say that it

would be a nice thing; however, I now know that this is
a tool used by sociopaths.

 A sociopath will pay close attention to your wants,
needs, desires, problems, famiy, upbringing, and other
things – everything about you. This isn't to get to "know
you." This is to use against you, manipulate you, and
gaslight you at a later date.

So, there I was – halfway back to my own family's home
and headed to restart my life once again. All of the
emotions flooding through my mind and heart were
overwhelming. He was feverishly trying to talk me into
going back. Then, he said it. After over a year of being
engaged with no discussions of an actual wedding he
said, "Let's just get married." I broke. He knew exactly
what to say to me. I turned around and headed back to
him. We were married two weeks later.

The rollercoaster was loaded and ready to go. I had no
idea what I was really in store for at all. I landed a job
at a large corporation and began my career. He had his
business, then another business, then another. I

handled the paperwork for his businesses while also working full time. He wasn't consistent in his businesses. He would work really hard and put a lot of money into them. He'd slowly lose interest and would just go in randomly. They were always businesses that required no employees at that point. Over the years he'd have several businesses – never lasting more than a year. The amount of money lost on these failed businesses were in the millions. However, it was his family's money. He never cared. They kept just handing over money to him to keep him occupied. They created a World just for him with no consequences from the failures.

🚩   A key trait of a sociopath is inconsistency in life. Rarely do they keep the same job with the same company for an extended part of time. They usually eventually let their guards down and begin to display their sociopathic behavior at work.

I am opting to not go into detail about the ins and outs of being in a relationship or marriage to a purported sociopath. Many things haunt me. But, one thing that haunts me often is that first day of meeting his parents His Mother – at the Chinese buffet – and her whisper. Years later it clicked out of nowhere. What did she whisper to me all of those years ago? "You know he's not normal, huh?" Understanding that silent whisper could've opened up the conversation that I needed to hear. Those 6 words could've changed the course of my life. Those 6 words could've led to me knowing that he was a high school dropout and had been put in two mental institutions prior to me even meeting him. Yet, those revelations didn't come until years later. Years after we were married and had children. Years after the abuse had crept in. Years after watching his parents enable him and ignore what they knew their son really was and the things he did. He was my problem now and they (mostly) had the peace of him having a scapegoat and "punching bag" other than themselves.

I can't change my past. All I can do is have faith that I will eventually recover from all of this. All I can do is hope that the right person picks up this book because peaked their interest. I hope that I can save just one person from the destruction, heartache, abuse, and life altering situations that I've been through – living nearly silently through it – all of these years.

The best advice I have is to get out – as soon as possible. If not, you can expect lying, cheating, manipulation, controlling behavior, projecting, gaslighting, violence, abuse (verbal, physical, sexual, mental, and financial), and much more. Sociopaths have no boundaries. They will attempt to destroy you in the end. They will leave you in a pile of ashes and move on to their next victim. At that point, you will be grateful and very lucky to have them move on to someone else. The pain will never leave you. Therapy and understanding are the best solutions to recovery.

RED FLAGS:

LEARN THEM
KNOW THEM
RUN FROM THEM

FREE ONLINE RESOURCES:

www.womenagainstabuse.org

www.benefits.gov

www.womenshealth.gov

Please also check with your private physician

and/or local government for resources available to you

www.ingramcontent.com/pod-product-compliance
Lightning Source LLC
Chambersburg PA
CBHW040306240726
48664CB00006B/1395